DINOSAURS

Written by Paul Stevenson

CONTENTS

Terrible Lizards	4
Living Large	6
Murderous Meat-Eaters	8
King Lizard	10
Claws of Death	12
Terror in the Sky	14
Monsters of the Deep	16
Awesome Armor	18
Boneheads	20
Secret Weapons	22
Not So Scary	24
What Happened to the Dinosaurs?	26
Record-Breakers	28
Working with Dinosaurs	30
Glossary	31
Index	32

First published in 2026 by
Hungry Tomato Ltd
F15, Old Bakery Studios, Blewetts Wharf, Malpas Road,
Truro, Cornwall, TR1 1QH, UK.

Thanks to our editor, Julie Tofflemire.

Copyright © 2026 Hungry Tomato Ltd

No part of this publication may be reproduced, stored in a retrieval system, or transmitted in any form or by any means, electronic, mechanical, photocopying, recording, or otherwise, without prior written permission of the copyright owner.

A CIP catalog record for this book is available from the British Library.

ISBN 9781835694466

Manufactured in the USA

Discover more at
www.hungrytomato.com

Neither the publisher nor the author shall be liable for any bodily harm or damage to property whatsoever that may be caused or sustained as a result of conducting any of the activities featured in this book.

All words in **BOLD** can be found in the glossary.

TERRIBLE LIZARDS

Dinosaurs ruled as the supreme land animals for more than 165 million years.

Dinosaurs first appeared between 200 million and 250 million years ago. They died out about 65 million years ago, long before humans were around. This period, called the Mesozoic Era, was dominated by dinosaurs.

The name "dinosaur" comes from Greek words meaning "terrible" and "lizard". Dinosaurs came in all shapes and sizes, from huge treetop-nibbling plant-eaters to chicken-sized hunter-killers.

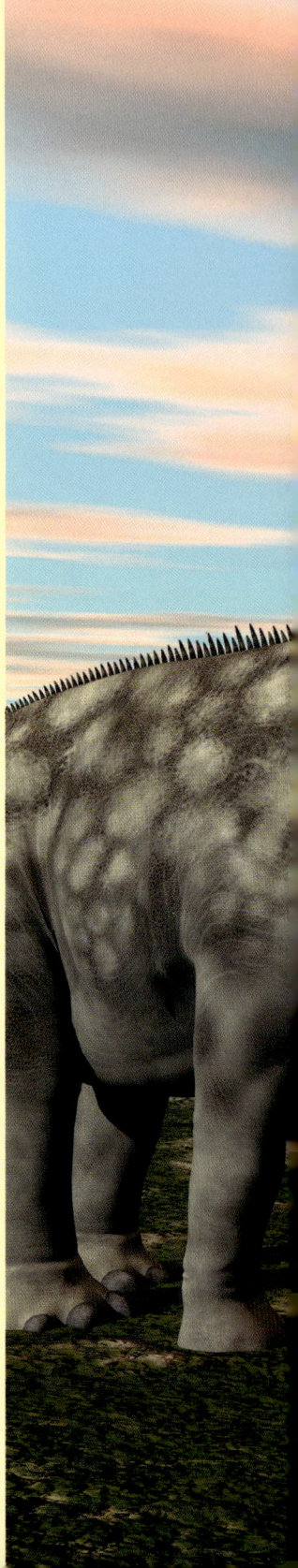

LIVING LARGE

The biggest land animals to ever exist were a group of plant-eating dinosaurs called sauropods.

Sauropods had long necks, small heads, enormous bodies, and four thick legs. They used their long necks to reach leaves that other animals couldn't.

One sauropod, Brachiosaurus, was about as tall as a four-story building! It weighed up to 176,000 pounds (80 tonnes)!

Brachiosaurus

Apatosaurus had a more horizontal posture than Brachiosaurus, making it sturdier. It had one claw on each front foot and three on each back foot.

The bones of its 50-foot (15-meter) neck were lightened thanks to small holes that made space for air.

An Apatosaurus skeleton

MURDEROUS MEAT-EATERS

Life for meat-eating dinosaurs could be tough – if they wanted dinner, they had to hunt down and kill it first!

Spinosaurus was about the length of three African elephants!

It had a large sail on its back. This may have been useful in maintaining body temperature, attracting a **mate**, or scaring other animals.

Spinosaurus

Allosaurus

Although Allosaurus was a **carnivore**, it probably wasn't a bone-cruncher like Tyrannosaurus rex.

Some scientists believe it used the powerful muscles in its neck to slam its head down on **prey** like a **hatchet**. It would then tear away flesh from its victim.

KING LIZARD

Tyrannosaurus rex, commonly known as T. rex was one of the fiercest dinosaurs around. No wonder its name means "King of the Tyrant Lizards"!

Tyrannosaurus rex

T. rex was 40 feet (12 meters) of muscle, claws, and teeth.

Its mouth was lined with **serrated** teeth that were around 7.5-12 inches (19-30.5 centimeters) long. It could open wide enough to swallow a six-year-old human in one gulp!

T. rex was powerful, but it wasn't built for speed. Some estimates suggest its top speed was only about 12 miles per hour (19.3 kilometers per hour). So, a human in good shape could probably have outrun a T. rex!

Instead of running after its own prey, it may have scared quicker **predators** away from their kill. Another theory is that it approached prey by **stealth** and pounced.

T.rex skeleton

CLAWS OF DEATH

For a long time, scientists believed that dinosaurs were slow and a bit stupid. But they were in for a shock when they discovered a new predator!

Deinonychus was unearthed in Montana, USA, in 1964. It was speedy, big-brained, and obviously vicious. They gave it a name meaning "terrible claw".

The claws on Deinonychus' back feet were around 5 inches (13 centimeters) long. A kick from this deadly weapon could slice open the belly of large prey. It also had more claws on its "hands" and arms.

Hand bones of a Deinonychus

The ferocious Deinonychus was slightly taller than an average adult human. The Velociraptor was related to the Deinonychus but was a lot smaller. Despite its size it was very intelligent and quick.

Velociraptor

TERROR IN THE SKY

Pterosaurs weren't technically dinosaurs, but they were still big and scary. They dominated the skies before birds and bats arrived on the scene.

Pterosaurs (pronounced without the "p") were **reptiles**, but they had wings and could fly. Some had a **wingspan** of up to 39 feet (12 meters) – almost as wide as an F-22 fighter jet! Others were smaller than a paper airplane.

Pteranodon

Rhamphorhynchus

The seagull-sized Rhamphorhynchus was one of the first pterosaurs, and it had a diamond-shaped **rudder** at the end of its tail.

Some pterosaurs' beaks had hundreds of thin, needle-like teeth. Scientists believe these could have been used to strain out **plankton** from the water or for stabbing fish.

MONSTERS OF THE DEEP

While dinosaurs ruled the land, some reptiles returned to life in the sea. They adapted to hunting many kinds of sea life.

Because they were not fish, sea reptiles had to come to the surface to breathe air.

At up to 43 feet (13 meters) long, Elasmosaurus would have been a scary sight. It ate fish, crabs, and **mollusks**. It may have held its head above the waves to surprise any curious fish with a sudden strike from above.

Elasmosaurus

Around 1811, two children – Mary Anning and her brother, Joseph – found the first Ichthyosaur **fossil**. Mary was only 12 at the time!

The fossil, which was 17 feet (5.2 meters) long, looked like a very big dolphin with a pointy beak.

Ichthyosaur

AWESOME ARMOR

In such a dangerous world, plant-eaters had to develop a range of special defenses to avoid being everyone else's lunch.

The most heavily armored animal ever to walk the Earth was Ankylosaurus.

The bony plates along its back had studded spikes, and the plates joined together to form an **impenetrable** shield, like a tortoise's shell.

Ankylosaurus

Triceratops had three horns on its face, two of which were about 3 feet (1 meter) long! It also had a large, bony frill at the back of its skull that protected its neck.

Triceratops

Stegosaurus had bony plates along its back. Scientists once thought these were used for defense, but now they think the plates helped it stay the right temperature. But Stegosaurus still had four big spikes on its tail to fight back!

Stegosaurus

BONEHEADS

Some dinosaurs had such strange skulls that scientists are still trying to figure out what they were meant to do!

A Pachycephalosaurus skull

Pachycephalosaurus had a bizarre dome-shaped head that was 9 inches (23 centimeters) thick in some places and had spikes and bony knobs sticking out.

The dome looks like a battering ram. However, it may have simply been used for **species** recognition or as a display feature.

Parasaurolophus is recognized by its long crest, which was **hollow**. It may have been used for a variety of purposes, including making loud sounds.

Parasaurolophus crest

Corythosaurus bony crest

Corythosaurus got its name – "helmet lizard" – from the semi-circular bony crest on its head.

Some scientists suggested it was a kind of **snorkel**! Other, more likely, theories include giving Corythosaurus a better sense of smell.

SECRET WEAPONS

Dinosaurs found some very inventive ways to defend themselves against attackers.

Giant sauropods, such as Diplodocus, had long tails to help balance their amazing necks. The stiff, bony end made a very effective whip to flick at predators.

For an even deadlier blow, some dinosaurs, like Ankylosaurus and Stegosaurus, could have used their spiky tails as a club.

Diplodocus

Iguanodon had a giant thumb spike on each hand. The spikes were probably a great defensive weapon. They may have also been useful for stripping tree branches or breaking into seeds.

Some dinosaurs, like Triceratops, may have lived in **herds**. If so, this would have offered some protection from predators.

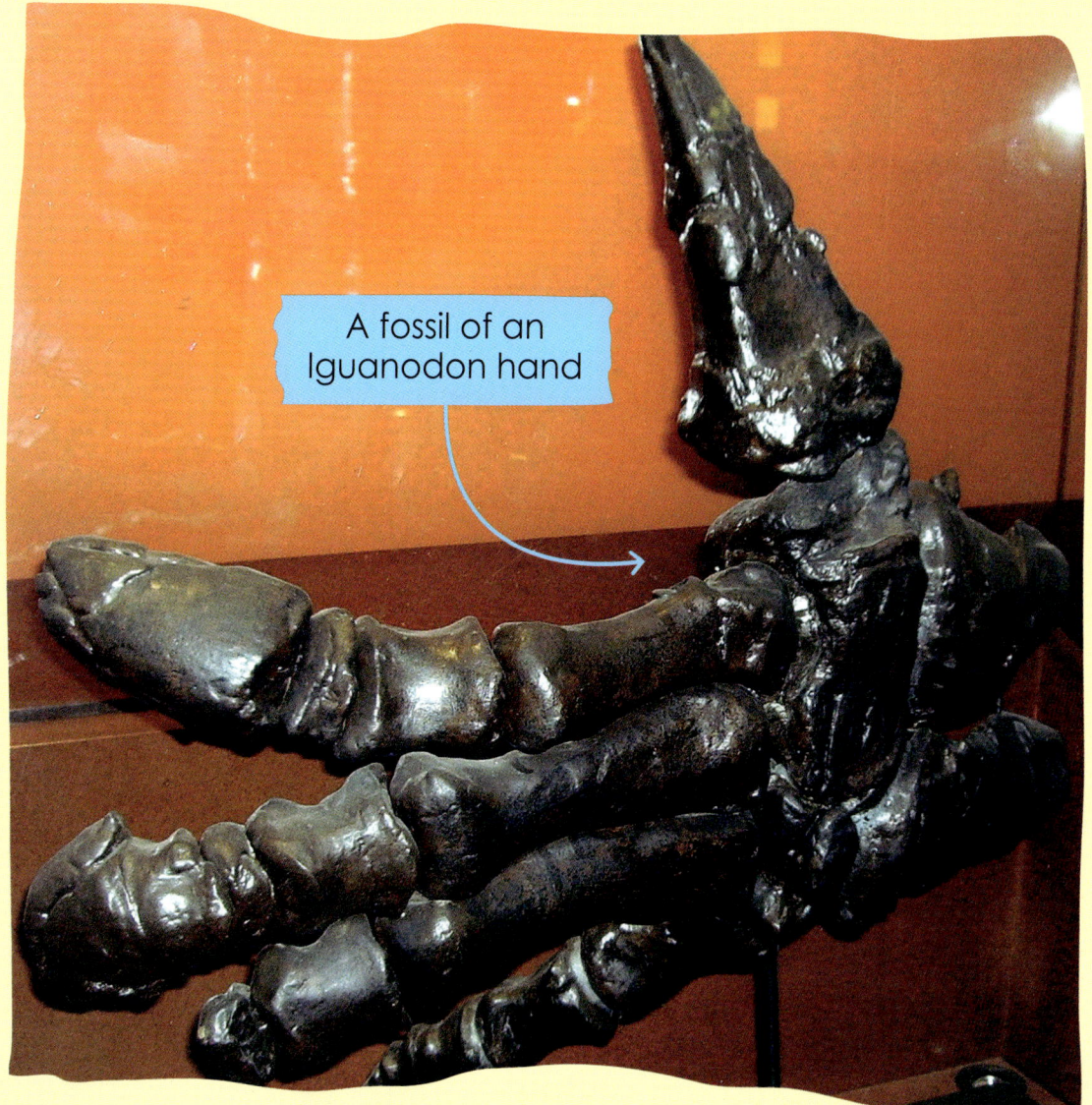

A fossil of an Iguanodon hand

NOT SO SCARY

Paleobiologists are people who study the bones of animals to find out how they lived. They can tell from fossils that some dinosaurs weren't scary at all.

Most dinosaurs were, in fact, plant-eaters (**herbivores**). They would only be a threat if you were a leaf!

Dinosaurs often buried their eggs and left their young to fend for themselves. Fossils from a Maiasaura nesting site showed that this dinosaur took good care of its **offspring** after they hatched. No wonder its name means "good mother lizard"!

Maiasaura

Reconstruction of a nest with eggs

The biggest ever claws belonged to Therizinosaurus. You might think this made it a fierce predator, but its head was small and it had no teeth!

These mysterious claws were probably just used for scratching at **termite** mounds.

Therizinosaurus

WHAT HAPPENED TO THE DINOSAURS?

There are still a lot of questions about the sudden extinction of dinosaurs and other creatures 65 million years ago.

There are all kinds of theories, but most scientists believe that an **asteroid** hit the Earth at that time.

It's estimated that the asteroid was traveling at 40,000 miles per hour (64,000 kph)! The impact instantly **vaporized** the rock around it.

The strong force triggered massive earthquakes and **tsunamis.**

Smoke and ash filled the air, blocking out much of the light for months... maybe even years! The drop in global temperatures would have made it hard for plants and animals to survive.

Volcanic eruptions might have also contributed to the mass extinction of the dinosaurs. One thing's for sure – they're gone!

RECORD-BREAKERS

In the dinosaur world, it's not easy to be the best, but these dinosaurs were unbeatable!

LARGEST DINOSAUR: ARGENTINOSAURUS

Argentinosaurus

Paleontologists haven't found a complete skeleton of Argentinosaurus yet. But based on the bones they do have, its estimated size is between 120-131 feet (37-40 meters).

SMALLEST DINOSAUR: OCULUDENTAVIS

Oculudentavis, whose name means "eye-tooth bird", was about the size of a hummingbird!

Hummingbird

FASTEST DINOSAUR: STRUTHIOMIMUS

Struthiomimus

One of the fastest dinosaurs was Struthiomimus, which reached speeds of up to 50 miles per hour (80 kph). Its name, which means "ostrich-mimic", is a perfect fit!

MOST TEETH: NIGERSAURUS

Nigersaurus

The Nigersaurus had 500 active teeth as well as replacements. Now that's something to smile about!

STRONGEST BITE FORCE: T.REX

Tyrannosaurus rex

With a bite force making up to 6 US tons (5.4 tonnes) of pressure, Tyrannosaurus rex's chomp was powerful enough to crush a car!

WORKING WITH DINOSAURS

Paleontologists study the fossils of living things from long ago. What do you need to become a paleontologist?

- A strong science background, usually all the way to the top level
- A curious mind so you can ask the right questions
- Strong problem-solving skills to find the right answers
- Physical endurance for fieldwork
- A love of dinosaurs, of course!

GLOSSARY

asteroid – small space rocks that orbit the Sun.

carnivore – a meat-eating animal.

fossil – a very old part of a plant or animal that has turned into rock.

hatchet – a small axe used for chopping.

herbivores – plant-eating animals.

hollow – to have a hole or empty space inside.

herds - a large group of animals that live together.

impenetrable – something that cannot be broken through or entered.

mate – the partner that an animal has babies with.

mollusks – creatures with soft bodies such as snails, slugs, and clams.

offspring – the young of an animal.

plankton – tiny living things that float around in water.

predators – animals that hunt and kill other animals.

prey – an animal that is hunted by other animals for food.

reptiles - a group of cold-blooded animals with backbones. Most reptiles lay eggs. Snakes, lizards, and dinosaurs are all reptiles.

rudder – used for steering and changing direction.

serrated – having sharp points in a line like the edge of a saw.

snorkel – a tube used for breathing through when your head is underwater.

species – a group of living things that share characteristics and features, and can have babies together.

stealth – quiet and secret movement or action.

termite – a small insect that eats wood and lives in groups called colonies.

tsunamis – huge waves in the sea, often caused by earthquakes.

vaporized – turned into gas.

wingspan – the measurement of one tip of a bird's or aircraft's wing to another.

INDEX

A
allosaurus 9
ankylosaurus 18, 22
anning, Mary and Joseph 17
apatosaurus 7
argentinosaurus 28
asteroid 26

B
brachiosaurus 6, 7

C
carnivore 9, 31
corythosaurus 21

D
deinonychus 12, 13
dinosaurs 4, 6, 8, 10, 12, 14, 16, 20, 22, 23, 24, 26, 27, 28, 29, 30
diplodocus 22

E
earthquakes 27
elasmosaurus 16, 17
elephants 8

F
fish 15, 16
fossils 17, 23, 24, 30, 31

H
herbivores 24, 31
humans 4, 10, 11, 13, 17
hummingbird 28

I
ichthyosaur 17
iguanodon 23

M
maiasaura 24
mate 8, 31
mollusks 31

N
nigersaurus 29

O
oculudentavis 28

P
pachycephalosaurus 20
paleontologists 28, 30
parasaurolophus 21
plankton 15, 31
predator 11, 12, 22, 23, 25, 31
pteranodon 14
pterosaurs 14, 15

R
reptiles 14, 16, 31
rhamphorhynchus 15

S
sauropods 6, 22
spinosaurus 8
stegosaurus 19, 22
struthiomimus 29

T
therizinosaurus 25
triceratops 19, 23
tsunami 27, 31
tyrannosaurus rex 9, 10, 11, 29

V
velociraptor 13

Picture credits:
(t=top; b=bottom; m=middle; l=left; r=right):
Shutterstock: AKKHARAT SARUSILAWONG 20m; Alberto Andrei Rosu 19t; Autumn Sky Photography 30b; Daniel Eskrigde 9t, 14bg, 21m, 22b, 24t, 25b; Dotted Yeti 4, 17m, 16-17bg; Elenarts 4-5bg, 12b, 19b, 21bl; Herschel Hoffmeyer 29tl; Jaime Calderon 13t; Kikujungboy CC 11b; Michael Rosskothen 15t; Orla 1bg, 2-3bg, 18b; Romana Edwards 28br; Romolo Tavani 26-27bg; Sammy 33 6-7bg, 28m; Schusterbauer.com 7mr; Ton Ponchai 27mr; Warpaint 8b, 10m, 29bl; William Cushman 29ml. Wikipedia: By Fernando Losada Rodríguez - Own work, CC BY-SA 4.0, https://commons.wikimedia.org/w/index.php?curid=4939486 24mr; By Credit to en:user:Ballista. Taken from the English wikipedia, uploaded here with the same licensing. - Own work, CC BY-SA 3.0, https://commons.wikimedia.org/w/index.php?curid=937289 23t; By James St. John - Deinonychus antirrhopus theropod dinosaur (Cloverly Formation, Lower Cretaceous; Carbon County, southern Montana, USA) 3, CC BY 2.0, https://commons.wikimedia.org/w/index.php?curid=35757293 12mr.

Every effort has been made to trace the copyright holders, and we apologize in advance for any unintentional omissions. We would be pleased to insert the appropriate acknowledgments in any subsequent edition of this publication.